Rejoice 'n' Sing

VOLUME I

COMPILED BY

Joanne Boyce, Chris Rolinson & Mike Stanley

FIRST PUBLISHED IN 1996

THIS BOOK COPYRIGHT © CJM MUSIC LTD
ISBN 0 12345 678 9

ALL SONGS COPYRIGHT © CJM MUSIC LTD

ALL RIGHTS RESERVED
Please do not reproduce any part of this book,
in any form, without the permission of the copyright holders.

ARTWORK
COVER by DEBBIE COLBY
ILLUSTRATIONS by MARIANNE SCAHILL
Used by Permission

PRINTED IN GREAT BRITAIN

CJM MUSIC LTD
St Mary's House, Coventry Road, Coleshill
West Midlands B46 3ED

Foreword

MUSIC FOR A NEW GENERATION

The material contained in this book is the fruit of several years' work, the seed of which was sown at Soli House. (Soli House is a residential Youth Retreat Centre in Stratford-upon-Avon, with a rich tradition of vibrant liturgy and music).

The first music release from Soli House was 'Lead Kindly Light' in 1991, which Largely featured the work of Mike Stanley who was working at Soli House at the time. Eighteen months after Mike's departure from the centre Joanne Boyce led the Soli House Team of '92 -'93 in the production of 'Earth Calling Heaven'. The third album, 'Bread of Life', released in 1994, combined the talents of both Jo and Mike, and was successful enough to encourage them to continue working together.

In October of 1994 Mike and Jo met Chris Rolinson and so was born the Christian music team Rolinson, Boyce & Stanley and their company CJM Music. The team began work on a new album, 'Imagine a World' and this music collection, 'Rejoice & Sing. Vol. I', for release in July 1996.

The songs in this book have already proved popular with young and old alike, across the Archdiocese of Birmingham and beyond. Hopefully this and future books will prove a valuable resource for the many groups who long to "sing a new song to the Lord".

Contents

IN BOTH 'The Words' AND 'The Music' SECTIONS EACH
SONG HAS THE SAME NUMBER, AS LISTED BELOW...

1 Ave Verum Corpus
    From the album 'Imagine a World'
    Contemporary setting of the traditional Latin text for Communion.
    Four part SATB arrangement works well un-accompanied.

2 Bread of Life
    From the album 'Bread of Life'
    Also available on CD 'Again I say Rejoice'
    A beautiful Communion song which encapsulates
    the essence of Eucharist.

3 Burntwood Mass - Penitential Rite
    From the album 'Imagine a World'
    A simple setting which may be sung in unison
    or as 'call and response'.

4 Burntwood Mass - Glory to God
    A lively setting of the Gloria.
    Verses can be sung in unison or as 'call and response'.

5 Burntwood Mass - Holy, Holy
    From the album 'Imagine a World'

6 Burntwood Mass - Memorial Acclamation
    From the album 'Imagine a World'
    Set to the same melody as the Burntwood Mass Penitential Rite.

7 Burntwood Mass - Great Amen
    From the album 'Imagine a World'
    A suitably triumphant refrain, especially enjoyed by young people.

8 Burntwood Mass - Lamb of God
    Gentle, reflective setting of the Agnus Dei

9 Come let us go
    From the album 'Bread of Life'
    Also available on the CD 'Again I say Rejoice'
    A lively Gathering song.

10 Dying you destroyed our Death
    From the album 'Bread of Life'
    Memorial Acclamation

11   He is Lord
From the album 'Bread of Life'
Also available on the CD 'Again I say Rejoice'
Gospel style re-working of the popular traditional
hymn 'Praise my soul the King of Heaven'.
Verses of other hymns and psalms may be set to the melody.

12   I am the Voice
From the album 'Lead Kindly Light'
Also available on the CD 'Again I say Rejoice'
Based on Luke 3:3-18. Especially suitable during Advent.

13   Lead Kindly Light
From the album 'Lead Kindly Light'
Also available on the CD 'Again I say Rejoice'
Inspired by the words of Cardinal Newman (1801-1890)

14   Lord, by your Cross
From the album 'Imagine a World'
A setting of the Memorial Acclamation and a powerful song in its own right.

15   Lord, let your Peace come
From the album 'Imagine a World'
Sign of Peace.

16   Magnificat
From the album 'Imagine a World'
A moving and uplifting setting that can be used as a
Responsorial Psalm or meditation piece.

17   Mistakes
From the album 'Bread of Life'
Also available on the CD 'Again I say Rejoice'
Suitable for Penitential and Reconciliation services.

18   Now this Offering
From the album 'Bread of Life'
Offertory and Preparation of Gifts

19   Our Father (Your Kingdom Come)
From the album 'Bread of Life'
Also available on the CD 'Again I say Rejoice'
An exciting setting of the Lord's Prayer with a simple, driving melody.

20   Praise Him
From the album 'Earth Calling Heaven'
Also available on the CD 'Again I say Rejoice'

21   Prayer of St Teresa
From the album 'Imagine a World'
Based on the Prayer of St Teresa - 'Let nothing Trouble You'
A moving reminder to trust in God alone.

22 Pray for a Miracle
From the album 'Earth Calling Heaven'
Also available on the CD 'Again I say Rejoice' and the cassette single 'One World'
Expresses the need to pray, as well as work, for justice & peace in our world.

23 Rain down Saving Justice
From the album 'Imagine a World'
A look at Christ as the fulfilment of God's Plan of Salvation.

24 Soli Mass - Penitential Rite
From the album 'Bread of Life'
A simple, gently lilting Kyrie. Can be sung as call and response.

25 Soli Mass - Holy, Holy
From the album 'Bread of Life'
A triumphant setting of the unending Hymn of Praise
Also suitable for Palm Sunday processions.

26 Soli Mass - Memorial Acclamation
From the album 'Bread of Life'

27 Soli Mass - Lamb of God
From the album 'Bread of Life'

28 Song to the Trinity
From the album 'Bread of Life'
Beautiful lyrics set to the Irish Air Buchlanaaran

29 Source of Life
Offertory and Preparation of Gifts.
Especially suitable for Maundy Thursday

30 When
From the album 'Imagine a World'
A reminder that God is always close, even in times of difficulty and doubt.

31 You are Worthy
From the album 'Imagine a World'
Praise of the wonderful works of God, from Creation to the Incarnation.

32 You came to heal
Penitential Rite

33 You know me
From the album 'Bread of Life'
Also available on the on the CD 'Again I say Rejoice'
Inspired by Jeremiah 1:5 "Before I formed you in the womb I knew you..."

The Words

1
Ave Verum Corpus
BY MIKE STANLEY

Ave verum corpus natum,
de Maria virgine.
Vere passum immolatum,
in cruce pro homine.
Cujus latus, perforatum
unda fluxit et sanguine.
Esto nobis, praegustatum
in mortis examine.

Hail to thee, true body of Christ;
Born of the Virgin, Mary;
Who suffered sacrifice for humankind;
whose side was pierce and flowed
with water and blood.
Be for us sustaining
in the throes of death.

2
Bread of Life
BY JOANNE BOYCE & MIKE STANLEY

Bread of life, truth eternal.
Broken now to set us free.
The risen Christ, his saving power,
is here in bread and wine for me.

Lord, I know
I am not worthy to receive you.
You speak the words and I am healed.
Here at your table, love's mystery;
One bread, one cup, one family.

Lord, by your cross
you reconciled us to the Father.
We have only to believe.
Your sacrifice, our victory.
Now by you blood we are redeemed.

Lord, you gave your people
manna in the desert.
Still, you fulfil our every need.
Lord, when we hunger;
Lord, when we thirst,
we come to you and we receive... the

3
Burntwood Mass ~ Penitential Rite
BY MIKE STANLEY & JOANNE BOYCE

You came to heal the broken hearted,
Lord, have mercy.
You came to call the lost and weary,
Christ have mercy.
You plead for us at God's right hand,
Lord, have mercy on us all;
have mercy on us all.

4
Burntwood Mass ~ Glory to God
BY MIKE STANLEY & JOANNE BOYCE

Glory, glory, glory to God on high!
Glory, glory, peace to all his people!

Lord, God our heavenly King;
Glory to God on high.
Almighty God and Father;
Glory to God on high.
We worship you, we give you thanks;
Glory to God on high.
We praise you for your glory.
Glory to God on high.

Jesus Christ, God's only Son;
Glory to God on high.
Have mercy on us, Lamb of God;
Glory to God on high.
Lord, you take away our sin;
Glory to God on high.
At the Father's right hand hear our prayer.
Glory to God on high.

For you alone are the Holy One; *Glory...*
You alone are the Lord, Most high;
Glory...
With the Holy Spirit; *Glory...*
In the glory of the Father. *Glory...*

5
Burntwood Mass - Holy, Holy
BY MIKE STANLEY

Holy, holy, holy, Lord of power,
Lord of might, your glory fills the earth.
Let the heavens cry out hosanna!

Holy, holy, holy, Lord of power,
Lord of might, your glory fills the earth.
Blessed is the one who comes
in the name of the Lord. Hosanna!

6
Burntwood Mass - Mem. Accl.
BY JOANNE BOYCE & MIKE STANLEY

Lord, by your cross and resurrection,
you redeem us.
Lord, by your cross and resurrection,
you have freed us.
and you will come again in glory,
you are the Saviour of the world,
the Saviour of the world.

7
Burntwood Mass - Great Amen
BY JOANNE BOYCE & MIKE STANLEY

Amen! Amen! *(Clap! Clap!)*
Let the heavens cry out hosanna!
Amen! Amen! *(Clap! Clap!)*
Let the heavens cry out hosanna! Amen!

8
Burntwood Mass - Lamb of God
BY JOANNE BOYCE & MIKE STANLEY

Lamb of God, you take away the sin of all
the world; have mercy on us, Lord.
Lamb of God, you take away the sin of all
the world; have mercy on us, Lord.
Lamb of God, you take away the sin of all
the world; Grant us peace.
(Lord, grant us peace.)

9
Come let us go
BY MIKE STANLEY

*Come let us go
up to the mountain of the Lord,
to the temple of his Holy Spirit.
Come let us go
up to the mountain of the Lord,
and glorify his holy name.*

Through noise and confusion
our witness shall be heard.
We raise our voices
to proclaim your holy word.

Heavenly Father,
receive my brokenness.
Change me, rearrange me,
restore my worthiness.

With banners lifted
we approach his glorious throne.
By graces gifted,
his power shall be known.

Zion, holy mountain,
we turn our eyes to you.
Lead us ever closer
in spirit and in truth.

10
Dying you destroyed our death
BY MIKE STANLEY

Dying you destroyed our death.
Riding you restored our life.
Lord, Jesus, we believe you will come,
will come again.

11
He is Lord
BY JOANNE BOYCE & MIKE STANLEY
Words by Henry Francis Lyte (1793-1847)

He is Lord! He is Lord! (4)

Praise my soul the King of heaven,
to his feet thy tribute bring.
Ransomed, healed, restored, forgiven.
Who like me his praise should sing.

Praise him for his grace and favour
to our Fathers in distress.
Praise him, still the same forever,
slow to chide and swift to bless.

Father-like he tends ad spares us,
well our feeble frame he knows.
In his hands he gently bears us,
rescues us from all our foes.

Angels help us to adore him,
ye behold him face to face.
Sun and moon bow down before him,
dwellers all in time and space.

12
I am the Voice
BY MIKE STANLEY

I am the voice crying out from the
wilderness, prepare a way for the Lord.
Open your heart and know his
forgiveness,
repent and believe in his Word.

(And) Why do you ask,
who is the one who sent me?
Why do you ask if I am the Christ?
For a greater one shall come
to be the redeemer.
Only he can be the saving light.

Then I saw the Spirit come down from the
heavens, descending in the form of a dove.
The dove descended low,
beside the flowing waters,
to rest upon the head of God's own Son.
Even today we can meet God in our hearts.
Even today we see the dove.
Don't be deceived, for if we believe
we receive the Father through the Son.

13
Lead Kindly Light
BY MIKE STANLEY & DOUG PARKER

Gently off'ring my self to you.
Giving myself in prayer.
Taking away all the fear and the doubt,
knowing that you are there.
Pushing away in a corner of shame,
the things that I know are wrong.
Gently off'ring myself to you,
speaking to you in song.

Lead kindly light, lead thou me on.
For only you know where I'm going.
Dark is the night without you by my side.
In you my soul finds rest.

Gently off'ring myself to you,
looking again for peace.
Leaning on you for the strength that I need,
begging my souls release.
Seeking new hope in a world of despair,
but knowing that you still care;
Gently off'ring myself to you,
giving myself in prayer.

14
Lord, by your Cross
BY CHRIS ROLINSON

Lord, by your cross and resurrection.
you set us free, you set us free.
Lord, by your cross and resurrection.
you set us free, you set us free.

You are the Saviour, the Saviour
the Saviour of the world.
You are the Saviour, the Saviour
the Saviour of the world.

15
Lord, let your peace come
BY JOANNE BOYCE & MIKE STANLEY

Lord, let your peace come.
Lord, let your will be done.
Voices hands and hearts united,
by your grace no more divided.
Abba, Father!
Lord, let your peace come.
(repeat with key change)

16
Magnificat
BY JOANNE BOYCE
Words adapted from Luke 46:1

*My soul glorifies the Lord,
my spirit rejoices
My God forever he will be,
bless his holy name.*

He looks upon me his servant,
Looks on me in my lowliness.
He works marvels for me,
hence forth all ages call me blessed,
call me blessed.

He scatters the proud hearted,
cast the mighty from their thrones.
His mighty arm before me,
in strength he raises the lowly,
raises the lowly.

He fills the starving with plenty,
but empty sends the rich away.
Frm age to age his mercy,
the mercy promised us forever,
promised forever.

17
Mistakes
BY TONY CUMMINGS & MIKE STANLEY

I let my mind go walking
down some distant road.
My foolish heart
thought it could run away.
But lately I have glimpsed a mighty hand
that holds a million lives
within its palm each day.

A shepherd will allow his sheep
to look for grass,
but some will leave,
they willfully will stray.
The shepherd knows that this will surely
come to pass, though he loves the ones
who go and those who stay.

*O we mistake the moment that we seize.
Mistake piled on mistake
by doing what we please.
But there's no mistaking love
we find on bended knees.
Mistakes, there's someone who can turn
them to opportunities*

My heart was hard,
my mind was slow, my life was fast.
My treasures lay in broken pots of play.
But now I find
the bad decisions of my past
God's using in an unexpected way.

I meet folk on the road
on which I used to be,
my own mistakes
help guide the words I say,
For my redeemer, and my friend,
is holding me, and he's reaching out

18
Now this offering
BY JOANNE BOYCE

Lord, creator of all, true Father of all,
blest and holy.
Through your goodness we bring,
this humble offering, make it worthy.
From human hands a sacrifice
that will become the bread of life.

Bread and wine we bring,
and lay before the table of the Lord.
And through this offering.
our worthiness restored.

All we are, Lord, is yours.
All we have now is yours, completely.
Like widow's mite these gifts we bring,
humble, selfless offering. Make us
worthy.
And may we through this mystery,
share in your divinity.

Our lives in offering,
we bring before the table of the Lord.
And through this offering,
our worthiness restored.

Bread and wine we bring....

19
Our Father (Your Kingdom Come)
BY MIKE STANLEY

Our Father, who art in heaven,
hallowed be you name.
Your kingdom come, your will be done
on earth as it is in heaven.

Give us this day our daily bread and,
forgive our weaknesses;
And those who fail us, trespass against us,
as you forgave let us forgive.

Deliver us from every evil,
Let us not be led astray.
Your kingdom come, you will be done,
as you taught us, Lord, we pray.

For the Kingdom, and the power
and the glory, Lord, are yours.
As they are today, will be tomorrow
and shall be forever more.

We sing amen, we lift our voices,
with the heavens we proclaim.
Your kingdom come, you will be done,
We cry 'Amen' in Jesus name!

Your kingdom come, your will be done.
We cry 'Amen' in Jesus name!

20
Praise Him
BY JOANNE BOYCE

Holy, holy,
filled with glory is the Lord, most high.
So gave him praise and sing,
Glory, glory!
How his love has touched my life,
touched my life and made me whole.

Now I just wanna
Praise him! Praise him!
Wanna pray it, shout it, sing it!
Praise him! Praise him!
Praise the Lord!

Mercy, Mercy!
I'm forgiven, now there's peace within.
So give him praise and sing.
Worthy, worthy!
The one who takes away my sin,
who's greater than him?
He is Lord of all!

21
Prayer of St. Teresa
BY CHRIS ROLINSON

Let nothing trouble you,
let nothing frighten you,
everything passes away.
Let nothing trouble you,
let nothing frighten you,
everything passes, God never changes,
patience obtains all.

Whoever has God wants for nothing.
Whoever has God has enough.
Whoever has God, has all they need
to live their life, for God alone will
suffice.

Let nothing trouble you,
let nothing frighten you,
everything passes away.
Let nothing trouble you,
let nothing frighten you,
everything passes, God never changes,
patience obtains all.

Whoever has God wants for nothing.
Whoever has God has enough.
Whoever has God, has all they need
to live their life, for God alone will

MIDDLE EIGHT
    Let nothing trouble you.
    Let nothing frighten you.
    Everything passes, God never changes.
    God never changes!

Whoever has God wants for nothing.
Whoever has God has enough.
Whoever has God, has all they need
to live their life, for God alone will
suffice.

22
Pray for a Miracle
BY JOANNE BOYCE

I prayed for peace,
I prayed a million times over.
I prayed for the release
of the many people who suffer.
I prayed for love between sister and
brother,
I prayed for a miracle.

I prayed for hope,
I prayed we'd all keep on trying
I prayed for time to save our world
from dying. I prayed for peace,
I prayed a million times over.
I prayed for a miracle.

Lord, in your mercy,
will you listen to my prayer.
Lord in your mercy,
lend this sinful child an ear.
Where two or three are gathered you said
that you'd be there, so I pray for a
miracle!

I prayed for the day
we'd all have justice and freedom.
I prayed that one day,
people in power would rule with wisdom.
And I prayed for the child with no one to
protect them. I prayed for a miracle!

Chorus

MIDDLE EIGHT
    The game of life is not so funny now.
    When will we find an answer?.
    When will we find a way?
    Cause all we do
    is build a house on sand,
    If we don't take time, take time,
    Take time to pray!

Pray for a miracle (4)

23
Rain down Saving Justice
BY MIKE STANLEY, RUTH MORRIS & PETER JOHNS

Rain down saving justice,
shower me from above.
Break through the clouds of
darkness Lord,
cover me with your love.

Your word is life
for all the broken hearted
if they will only turn their eyes to see,
beyond the many lies that separate us
from the glory of your majesty

The Son of God, crucified to save us.
His body broken, his spirit breaking free.
The Father's will,
the word sent to reclaim us
that we can stand forgiven now.

The Father's voice resounds
throughout the heavens.
The Spirits fire consumes the enemy.
The faithful ones,
washed in the blood of Jesus
Shall rise and claim his victory.

24
Soli Mass - Penitential Rite
BY JOANNE BOYCE,

Show mercy to us, loving Father.
We have sinned against you,
please make us anew.
In your love and your grace
you forgive us.
Lord, have mercy, Lord, have mercy.

Look not on our failings, Lord, Jesus.
We have sinned against you,
please make us anew.
By your life and your death
you redeem us.
Christ have mercy, Christ have mercy.

Come fill our hearts Holy Spirit.
We have sinned against you,
please make us anew.
Forgive us and heal us and save us.
Lord, have mercy; Lord, have mercy.

25
Soli Mass - Holy, Holy
BY JOANNE BOYCE,

Hosanna! Hosanna! (2)
Hosanna in the highest!

Holy is the Lord, God Almighty.
Heaven and earth are full of his glory.
Holy is the Lord. Holy is the Lord.
Holy is the name of the Lord.

Blest is he who comes in the Lord's name.
Heav'n and earth are full of his glory.
Blessed is the Lord. Bless is the Lord.
Blessed is the Lord. Blessed is the Lord.
Blessed is the name of the Lord.

26
Soli Mass - Memorial Accl.
BY JOANNE BOYCE,

We eat this bread, we drink this cup
and remember your life and your death.
Our saving Lord now lifted up
and we wait 'til you come..
 in glory *(Come, Lord Jesus)*.
Come in Glory *(Come, Lord Jesus)*.

27
Soli Mass - Lamb of God.
BY JOANNE BOYCE,

Jesus, Lamb of God, you take
away our sin. Show mercy, Lord. *(repeat)*
Jesus, Lamb of God,
you take away our sin.
Grant us peace, grant us peace,
grant us peace, grant us peace.

28
Song to the Trinity
BY MIKE STANLEY
Traditional Irish Air

Father, I know that your love
for me has no bounds.
When darkness has fallen
your voice from the heavens resounds.
Saying "Trust and believe"
"Come and walk on my road to its end".
Then take me home Father, Spirit and Son,
my master and friend.

Spirit, I know that your truth
is spoken each day.
But power and greed change the creed,
leaving truth to decay.
So let the heavens resound
with hosannas to you, Holy One.
For in you Father, Spirit and Son,
the battle is won.

Jesus, I know that your love
for me has no end.
My faith growing stronger each day
that on you I depend.
When my doubting subsides,
when I'm finally brought to my knees;
Through my prayer, Father, Spirit and Son,
your grace is revealed.

29
Source of Life
BY MIKE STANLEY

In these gifts we bring,
we honour you, our King.
With humble offering, we make our prayers to you.

That you would help us grow,
reap harvests that you sow;
in fullness come to know
the promise that you made.

*For in bread and wine you become for us
the source of life, our sacrifice.
For in bread and wine, you become for us,
the source of life, our sacrifice.
Our sacrifice.*

The night he was betrayed,
a covenant was made;
Our debt becoming paid
by the Father through the son.

This is why today,
with words of love we pray
through breaking read we may
receive the gift of life.

30
When
BY Fr. ED HONE CSsR & MIKE STANLEY

When the road is long and hard,
When I do not know the way.
When I'm cold and look for comfort,
at the closing of the day.
When I need a hand to guide me,
a strength that will not fail,
my friend, my friend
is standing close to me.

When I thirst for truth and justice,
When I long for what is right,
When I feel my health is failing,
When I dread cold death's night;
When I feel my life lacks meaning,
When I know I can't go on,
My Lord, my Lord is standing close to me.

When I see my neighbour's need,
but I look the other way;
When I feel so lost, so helpless,
When I can't find words to pray.
When see hatred and division,
a world crying out for peace,
Jesus, Jesus is standing close to me.

31
You are Worthy
BY CHRIS ROLINSON, JOANNE BOYCE & MIKE STANLEY

You are the Fountain of holiness,
Father of righteousness.
Great is you faithfulness.
You are worthy, worthy Lord.

Praise him! All nations,
all peoples bless his name
Yahweh, faithful and just.
Mighty, Lord above all.
From age to age proclaim.

Praise him!
Marvellous things he has done.
Creation, work of his hands.
Heaven, sun moon and stars.
From age to age proclaim.

Praise him!
For us the Word became flesh.
Jesus, his gift of love.
Given once and for all.
From age to age proclaim.

32
You came to heal
BY CHRIS ROLINSON
Words adapted

You came to heal the broken hearted
Lord, have mercy.
You came to call the lost and weary,
Christ, have mercy.
You plead for us at Father's right hand,
Lord, our Lord, have mercy,
have mercy on us.

Lord, have mercy. Lord, have mercy.
Have mercy, have mercy on us.

33
You know me
BY MIKE STANLEY

You know me, you formed me,
you gave me life.
From darkness you called me,
you changed my life.
And even as the sun sinks down,
I see you light shine through.
For still the stars of heaven shine
and I'm alive in you, alive in you.

You know me, you heal me,
you set me free.
You opened up your arms
and gave your life for me.
And though the skies were darkened
and the heavens torn apart,
for love your life had ended,
that in truth my life may start,
my life may start.

You know me, reach out
and take my emptiness.
Transform me and let me
share your holiness.
Thguh clouds my gather round me
when you seem so far away,
mould me in your image
as the potter moulds the clay,
moulds the clay.

You know me, I know you we are as one.
The old life has ended, the new begun.
For in the silent moments
in the sunrise, in the fields,
all creation sings in praise
and so you are revealed, you are revealed.

You know me, I'm alive in you,
alive in you. *(repeat to end)*

The Music

1
Ave Verum Corpus (SATB)

BY MIKE STANLEY
arr. Chris Rolinson

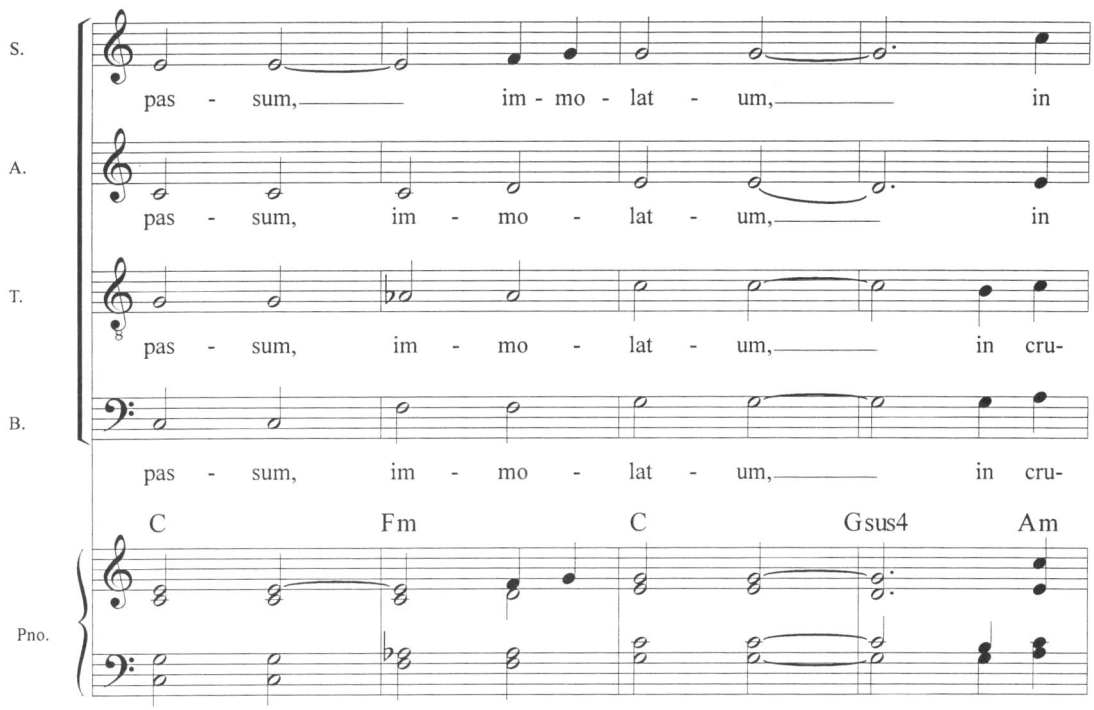

2
Bread of Life

BY JOANNE BOYCE & MIKE STANLEY
arr. Chris Rolinson

2. Lord, by your cross
   you reconciled us to the Father,
   We have only to believe.
   Your sacrifice, our victory
   Now by your blood we are redeemed,

3. Lord, you gave your people
   Manna in the desert
   Still you fulfil our every need.
   Lord, when we hunger, Lord, when we thirst,
   We come to you and we receive, (the)

3. Burntwood Mass - Penitential Rite

BY MIKE STANLEY & JOANNE BOYCE
arr. Chris Rolinson

4
Burntwood Mass ~ Glory to God

BY MIKE STANLEY & JOANNE BOYCE
arr. Chris Rolinson

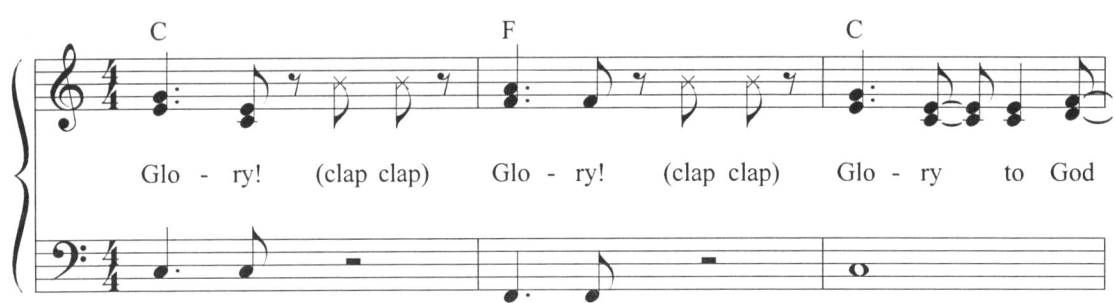

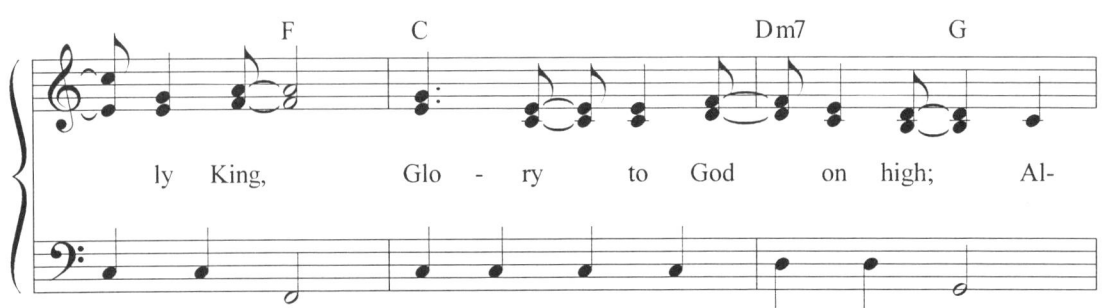

Copyright © 1995 CJM Music
ALL RIGHTS RESERVED

2. Jesus Christ, God's only Son, Glory...
   Have mercy on us, Lamb of God, Glory...
   Lord, you take away our sin, Glory...
   At the Father's right hand hear our prayer. Glory...

3. For you alone are the Holy One, Glory...
   You alone are the Lord, Most High. Glory...
   With the Holy Spirit, Glory....
   In the glory of the Father. Glory...

5
Burntwood Mass ~ Holy, Holy
BY MIKE STANLEY
arr. Chris Rolinson

Copyright © 1995 CJM Music
ALL RIGHTS RESERVED

6 Burntwood Mass - Memorial Acclamation

BY MIKE STANLEY & JOANNE BOYCE
arr. Chris Rolinson

Lord by your cross and re-surr-ect-ion, you re-deem us. Lord by your cross and re-surr-ect-ion, you have freed us, and you will come a-gain in glo-ry. You are the Sav-iour of the world, the Sav-iour of the world.

Copyright © 1995 CJM Music
ALL RIGHTS RESERVED

7
Burntwood Mass - Great Amen

BY MIKE STANLEY & JOANNE BOYCE
arr. Chris Rolinson

With joy and strength

Copyright © 1995 CJM Music
ALL RIGHTS RESERVED

8
Burntwood Mass ~ Lamb of God

BY MIKE STANLEY & JOANNE BOYCE
arr. Chris Rolinson

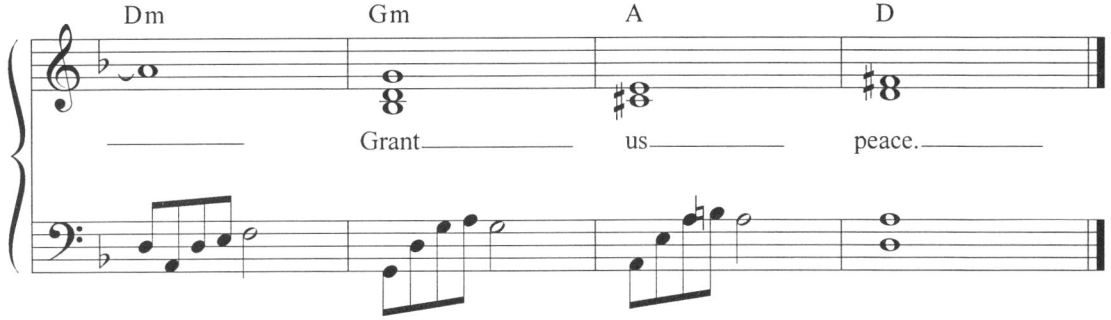

9
Come, let us go

BY MIKE STANLEY
arr. Chris Rolinson

40

2. Heavenly Father,
   Receive my brokeness.
   Change me, re-arrange me,
   Restore my worthiness.

3. With banners lifted
   We approach His glorious throne.
   By graces gifted,
   His power shall be known.

4. Zion, holy mountain,
   We turn our eyes to you,
   Lead us ever closer
   In spirit and in truth.

10
Dying you destroyed our Death

BY MIKE STANLEY
arr. Chris Rolinson

Copyright © 1995 CJM Music
ALL RIGHTS RESERVED

11
He is Lord!

JOANNE BOYCE & MIKE STANLEY
Words by Henry Francis Lyte 1793-1847
arr. Chris Rolinson

Copyright © 1995 CJM Music
ALL RIGHTS RESERVED

2. Praise him for his grace and favour,
   To our fathers in distress.
   Praise him, still the same forever,
   Slow to chide and swift to bless.

3. Father-like he tends and spares us,
   Well our feeble frame he knows.
   In his hands he gently bears us,
   Rescues us from all our foes.

4. Angels help us to adore him,
   Ye behold him face to face.
   Sun and moon bow down before him,
   Dwellers all in time and space.

12. I am the Voice

BY MIKE STANLEY
arr. Chris Rolinson

Copyright © 1995 CJM Music
ALL RIGHTS RESERVED

2. Then I saw the Spirit come down from the heavens,
   descending in the form of a dove.
   The dove descended low beside the flowing waters,
   to rest upon the head of God's own Son.

3. Even today, we can meet God in our hearts.
   Even today we see the dove.
   Don't be deceived, for if we believe,
   We receive the Father through the Son,

13 Lead, Kindly Light

BY MIKE STANLEY & DOUG PARKER
arr. Chris Rolinson

Copyright © 1995 CJM Music
ALL RIGHTS RESERVED

2. Gently offr'ing myself to you,
   Looking again for peace.
   Leaning on you for the strength that I need,
   Begging my soul's release.
   Seeking new hope in a world of despair,
   But knowing that you still care.
   Gently offr'ing myself to you,
   Giving myself in prayer.

14
Lord by your Cross (Saviour of the World)
BY CHRIS ROLINSON

15
Lord, Let Your Peace Come
BY JOANNE BOYCE & MIKE STANLEY
arr. Chris Rolinson

Gentle 'gospel' feel

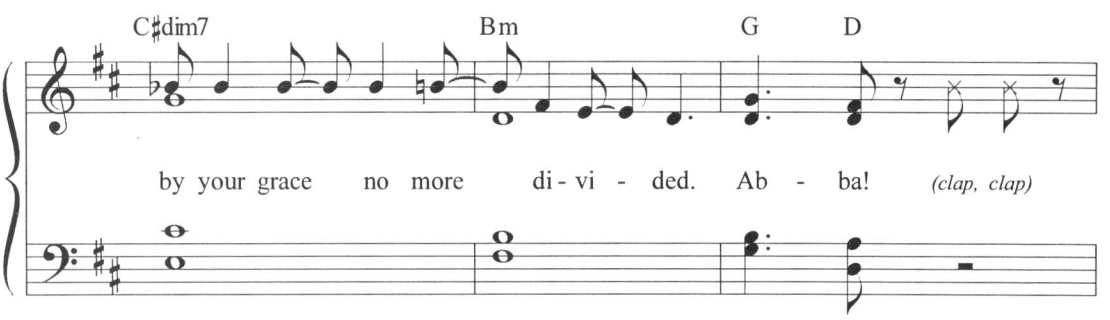

Copyright © 1995 CJM Music
ALL RIGHTS RESERVED

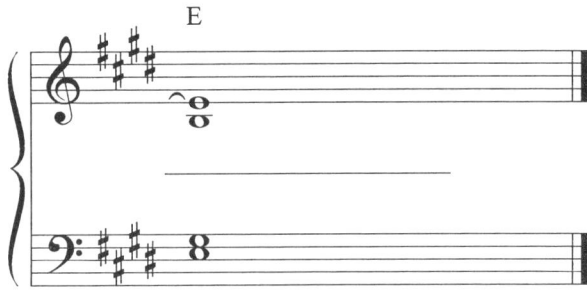

16 Magnificat

BY JOANNE BOYCE
arr. Chris Rolinson

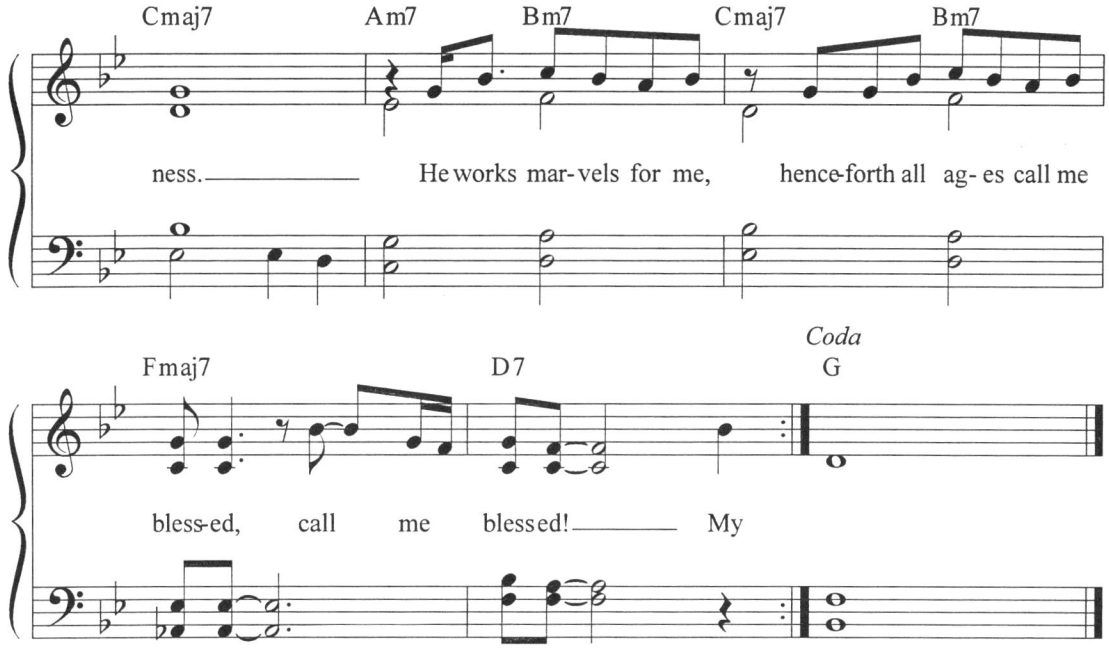

2. He scatters the proud-hearted,
   Cast the mighty from their thrones,
   His mighty arm before me,
   In strength he raises the lowly, raises the lowly!

3. He fills the starving with plenty,
   But empty sends the rich away,
   From age to age his mercy,
   The mercy promised us forever, promised forever!

17
Mistakes
BY MIKE STANLEY & TONY CUMMINGS
arr. Chris Rolinson

Copyright © 1995 CJM Music
ALL RIGHTS RESERVED

2. My heart was hard, my mind was slow, my life was fast;
   My treasures lay in broken pots of clay.
   But now I find the bad decisions of my past
   God's using in an unexpected way.
   I meet folk on the road on which I used to be,
   My own mistakes help guide the words I say,
   For my redeemer and my friend is holding me
   And he's reaching out to hold you too, today.

18. Now this Offering

BY JOANNE BOYCE
arr. Chris Rolinson

All we are, Lord, is yours,
   All we have now is yours,
   Completely.
   Like widow's mite these gifts we bring
   Humble, selfless offering
   Make us worthy.
   And may we, through this mystery,
   Share in your divinity.

Chorus 2
Our lives in offering,
We bring before the table of the Lord,
And through this offering,
Our worthiness restored.

Repeat chorus 1

19
Our Father (Your Kingdom Come)

BY MIKE STANLEY
arr. Chris Rolinson

With conviction and drive

Our Father, who art in heaven, hallowed be your name. Your kingdom come, your will be done, on earth as it is in heav'n. Give us this day our daily bread and forgive our weaknesses,

Copyright © 1995 CJM Music
ALL RIGHTS RESERVED

20 Praise Him

BY JOANNE BOYCE
arr. Chris Rolinson

2. Mercy, mercy!
I'm forgiven, now there's peace within.
So give Him praise and sing,
Worthy, worthy!
The one who takes away my sin,
Who's greater than him?
He is Lord of all!

21
Prayer of St Teresa
BY CHRIS ROLINSON

Copyright © 1995 CJM Music Ltd
ALL RIGHTS RESERVED

22
Pray for a Miracle

BY JOANNE BOYCE
arr. Chris Rolinson

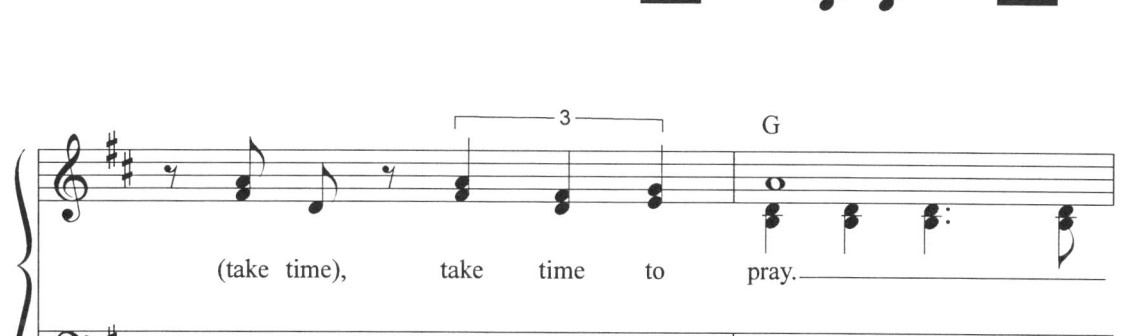

2. I prayed for hope, I prayed we'd all keep on trying.
   I prayed for time to save our world from dying.
   I prayed for peace, I prayed a million times over.
   I prayed for a miralce.

3. I prayed for the day we'd all have justice and freedom.
   I prayed that one day people in power would rule with wisdom.
   I prayed for the child with no-one to protect them.
   I prayed for a miracle.

   Lord, in your mercy will you listen to my prayer.
   Lord, in your mercy lend this sinful child a ear.
   Where two or three are gathered, we know that you are there,
   So we pray for a miracle.

23
Rain Down, Saving Justice

BY MIKE STANLEY, RUTH MORRIS & PETER JOHNS
arr. Chris Rolinson

Copyright © 1995 CJM Music Ltd
ALL RIGHTS RESERVED

2. The Son of God, crucified to save us,
   His body broken, his Spirit breaking free.
   The Father's will, the Word sent to reclaim us,
   That we can stand forgiven now.

3. The Father's voice resounds throughout the heavens,
   The Spirit's fire consumes the enemy.
   The faithful ones washed in the blood of Jesus
   Shall rise and claim his victory.

24
Soli Mass ~ Penitential Rite

BY JOANNE BOYCE
arr. Chris Rolinson

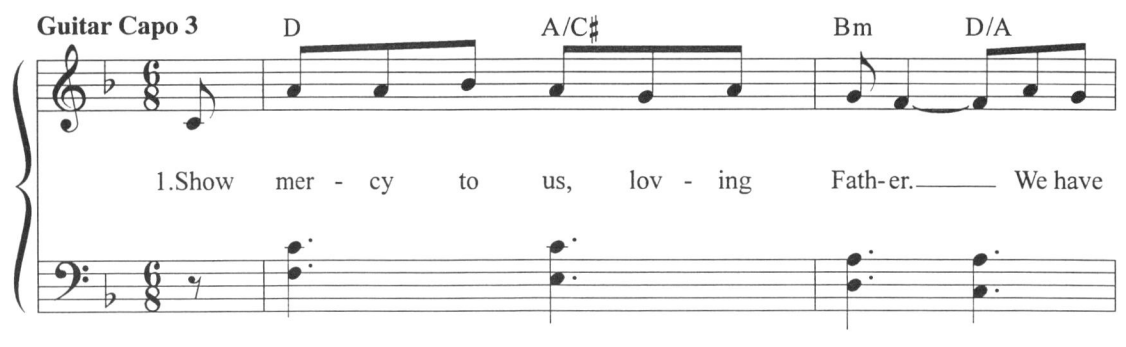

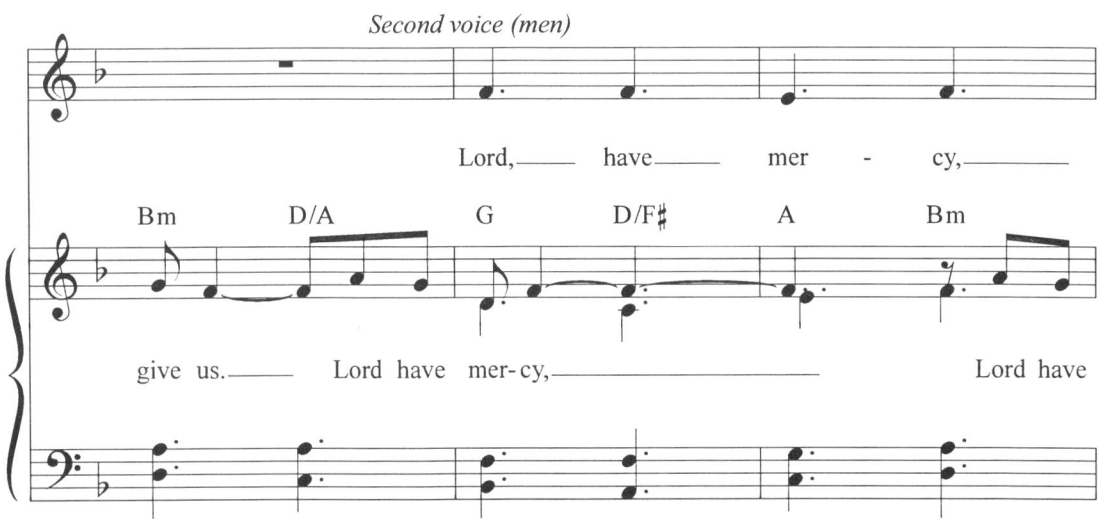

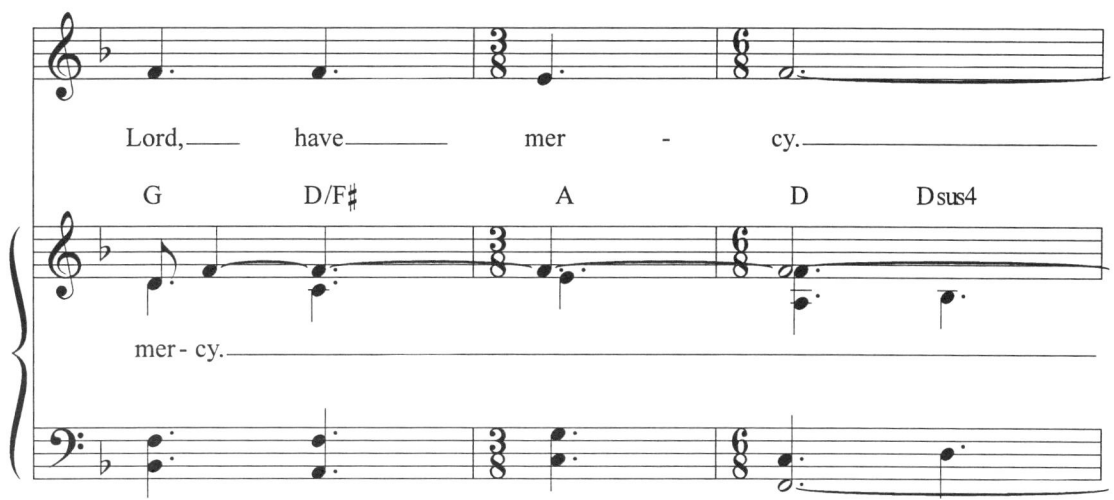

2. Look not on our failings, Lord Jesus.
   We have sinned against you,
   Please make us anew.
   By your life and your death you redeem us,
   Christ have mercy, Christ have mercy.

3. Come fill our hearts, Holy Spirit,
   We have sinned against you,
   Please make us anew,
   Forgive us and heal us and save us,
   Lord have mercy, Lord have mercy.

25
Soli Mass ~ Holy, Holy

BY JOANNE BOYCE
arr. Chris Rolinson

Copyright © 1995 CJM Music Ltd
ALL RIGHTS RESERVED

1. Ho-ly is the Lord, God al-migh-ty,
Heav'n and earth are full of his glo-ry.
Ho-ly is the Lord, ho-ly is the Lord,
ho-ly is the name of the Lord.

Ho-

2. Blest is he who comes in the Lord's Name.
Heav'n and earth are full of his glory.
Blessed is the Lord, blessed is the Lord,
Blessed is the name of the Lord.

85

26
Soli Mass ~ Memorial Acclamation

BY JOANNE BOYCE
arr. Chris Rolinson

Gently

We eat this bread, we drink this cup and re-mem-

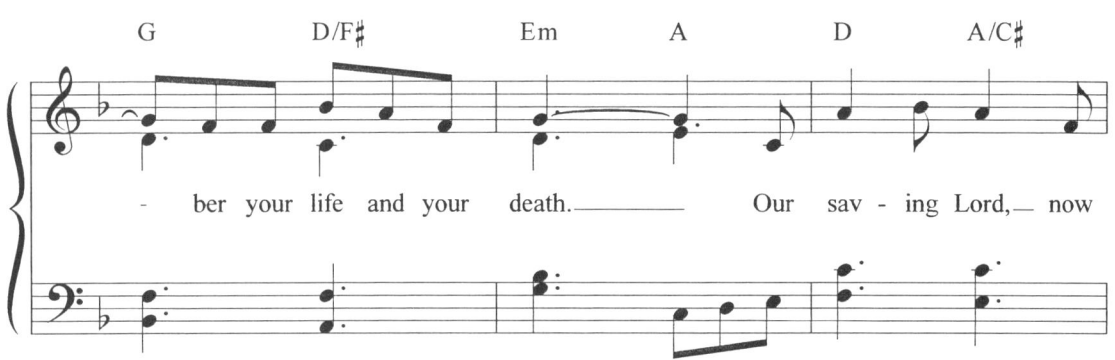

-ber your life and your death. Our sav-ing Lord, now

Second voice (men)

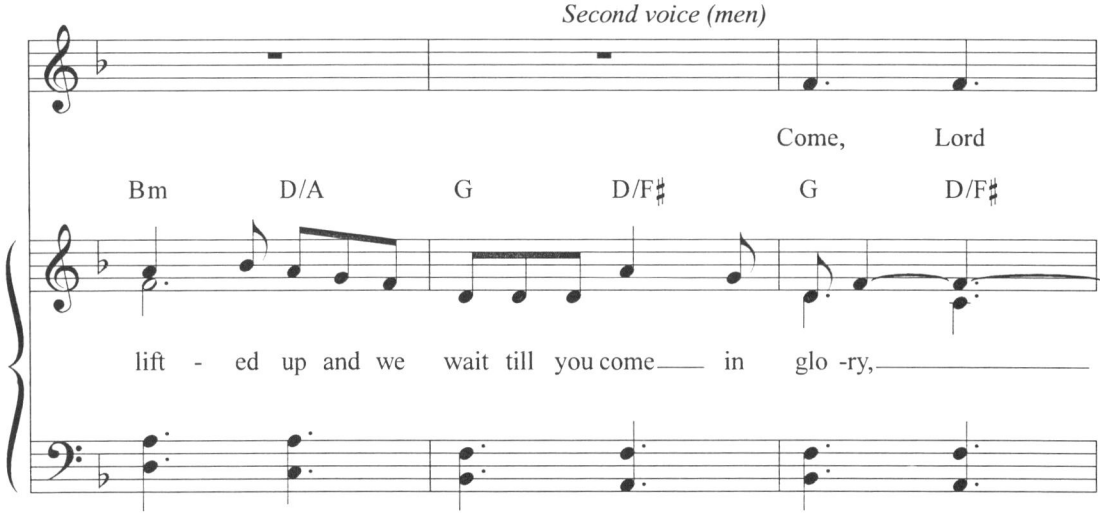

lift-ed up and we wait till you come in glo-ry,

Come, Lord

Copyright © 1995 CJM Music Ltd
ALL RIGHTS RESERVED

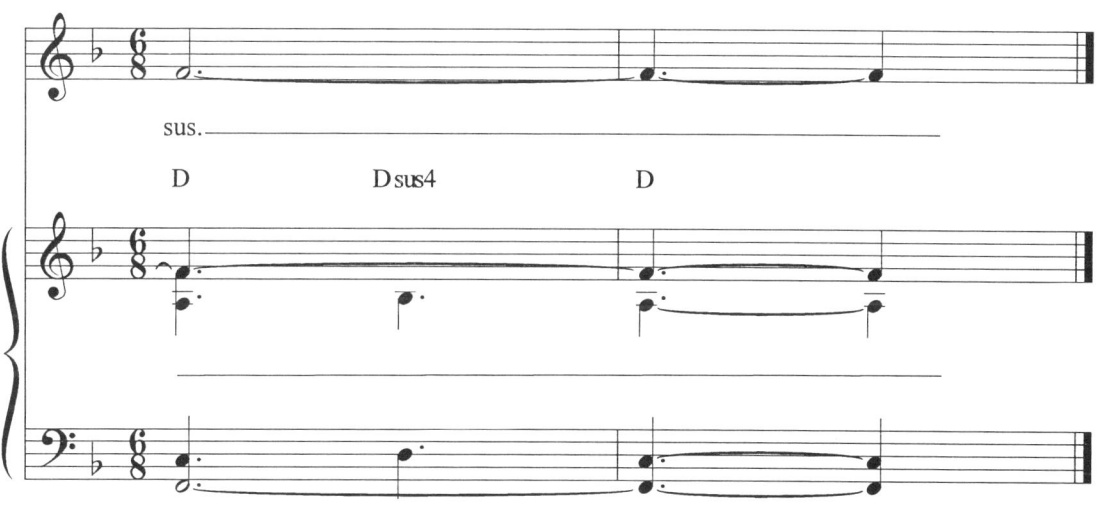

27
Soli Mass ~ Lamb of God

BY JOANNE BOYCE
arr. Chris Rolinson

Copyright © 1995 CJM Music Ltd
ALL RIGHTS RESERVED

28
Song to the Trinity

BY MIKE STANLEY
arr. Chris Rolinson

Copyright © 1995 CJM Music Ltd
ALL RIGHTS RESERVED

2. Spirit, I know that your truth
   is spoken each day.
   But power and greed change the creed
   leaving truth to decay.
   So let the heavens resound
   with 'Hosannas' to you, Holy One,
   For in you, Father, Spirit and Son
   the battle is won.

3. Jesus, I know that your love
   for me has no end.
   My faith growing stronger each day
   that on you I depend.
   When my doubting subsides,
   when I'm finally brought to my knees;
   Through my prayers, Father, Spirit and Son
   your grace is revealed.

29
Source of Life

BY MIKE STANLEY
arr. Chris Rolinson

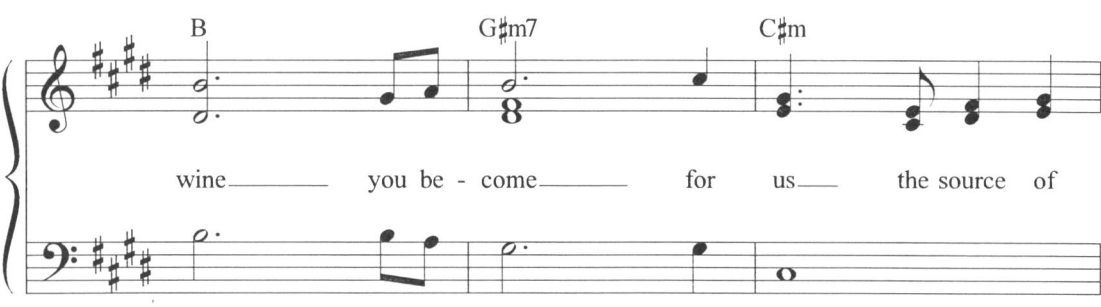

2. The night he was betrayed,
   a covenant was made;
   Our debt becoming paid
   by the Father through the Son.
   This is why today, with words of love we pray
   Through breaking bread we may
   receive the gift of life.

30
When

BY FR. ED HONE CSsR & MIKE STANLEY
arr. Chris Rolinson

2. When I thirst for truth and justice,
   When I long for what is right,
   When I feel my health is failing,
   When I dread cold death's night,
   When I feel my life lacks meaning,
   When I know I can't go on,
   My Lord, My Lord is standing close to me.

3. When I see my neighbour's need,
   But I look the other way,
   When I feel so lost, so helpless,
   When I can't find words to pray
   When I see hatred and division,
   A world crying out for peace,
   Jesus, Jesus is standing close to me.

31
You are Worthy
BY CHRIS ROLINSON, JOANNE BOYCE & MIKE STANLEY

Copyright © 1995 CJM Music Ltd
ALL RIGHTS RESERVED

2. Praise him!
   Marvellous things he has done.
   Creation, work of his hands.
   Heaven, sun, moon and stars,
   From age to age proclaim.

3. Praise Him!
   For us the Word became flesh.
   Jesus, his gift of love.
   Given once and for all,
   From age to age proclaim.

32
You came to heal
BY CHRIS ROLINSON

With Expression

You came to heal the broken hearted, Lord, have mercy. You came to call the lost and weary, Christ, have mercy. You plead for us at Father's right hand, O Lord, our Lord, have mercy, have mercy on

Copyright © 1995 CJM Music Ltd
ALL RIGHTS RESERVED

33
You Know Me

BY MIKE STANLEY
arr. Chris Rolinson

Sensitively

You know me, you formed me, you gave me life. From dark-ness you called me, you changed my life. And ev-en as the sun sinks down, I see your light shine through. For

Copyright © 1995 CJM Music Ltd.
ALL RIGHTS RESERVED

2. You know me, you heal me, you set me free.
   You opened up your arms and gave your life for me.
   And though the skies were darkened
   And the Heavens torn apart,
   For love your life had ended,
   That in truth my life may start, my life may start.

3. You know me, reach out and take my emptiness.
   Transform me and let me share your holiness.
   Though clouds may gather round me
   When you seem so far away;
   Mould me in your image
   As the potter moulds the clay, moulds the clay.

4. You know me, I know you, we are as one,
   The old life has ended, the new begun,
   For in the silent moments
   In the sunrise, in the fields,
   All creation sings in praise
   And so you are revealed, you are revealed.

ACKNOWLEDGMENTS

We have been blessed by support from a great many people, without whom CJM Music and our music ministry as it is now, may not have come to be. Our sincere gratitude goes to:

Fr Michael White, for his vision and inspiration; Soli House Teams - past and present; the Birmingham Catholic Youth Service; The Archdiocese of Birmingham and The Canticle Trust for practical and financial support; many friends and family, who have supported us beyond the call of duty.

When we formed CJM Music in October of 1994, we couldn't help but feel that we had been called together for a special purpose. Above all else, we thank God for that call, and for the gifts he has given us to realise our commitment to young people and the Church through music.

Mike Stanley
Joanne Boyce
Chris Rolinson
June 1996

CJM Music is committed to resourcing the provision of music for collective worship in schools and parishes; bringing vibrant, youthful liturgy not just to young people, but to the whole church.

- Writing and recording new liturgical and contemporary Christian music.

- Workshops and training for liturgy teams, choirs and music groups.

- Planning and leading music and animating worship for festivals, rallies, conferences, Masses etc.

- Staging concerts and other productions.